D1737960

# THE HILL

## A WALK THROUGH HISTORY

Joe DeGregorio

*Joe DeGregorio*

REEDY PRESS

Copyright © 2022. Reedy Press, LLC
All rights reserved.

Reedy Press
PO Box 5131
St. Louis, MO 63139
www.reedypress.com

No part of this publication may be reproduced or transmitted in any form or by any means, electronic or mechanical, including photocopy, recording, or any information storage and retrieval system, without permission in writing from the publisher.

All images believed to be in the public domain unless noted otherwise.

Permissions may be sought directly from Reedy Press at the above mailing address or via our website at www.reedypress.com.

Front cover inset images (l to r): Piazza fountain, Barbara Northcott; Vintage Missouri Baking Co, Mimi Lordo; Café Dolce, Tracy Duchinsky; Vintage Fassi Store, Paula Fassi; Yogi block BVM, Tracy Duchinsky.

Back cover images (l to r): Italian Heritage Parade, *St. Louis Post-Dispatch*; Pasta Challenge, Mama's on the Hill website; Vintge Oldani Salami, The Hill Neighborhood Center.

Design: Richard Roden
All images are courtesy of the author unless otherwise noted.

ISBN: 9781681064086

Printed in the United States

22 23 24 25 26 5 4 3 2 1

We (the publisher and the author) have done our best to provide the most accurate information available when this book was completed. However, we make no warranty, guaranty, or promise about the accuracy, completeness, or currency of the information provided, and we expressly disclaim all warranties, express or implied. Please note that attractions, company names, addresses, websites, and phone numbers are subject to change or closure, and this is outside of our control. We are not responsible for any loss, damage, injury, or inconvenience that may occur due to the use of this book. When exploring new destinations, please do your homework before you go. You are responsible for your own safety and health when using this book. Also note that some stops on this walk are currently occupied, private residences. Please be respectful and remain on the sidewalk.

# TABLE OF CONTENTS

# DEDICATION

This book is dedicated to my only grandchild, Henry DeGregorio, my favorite fan who has exhibited great interest in my previous contributions, including *The Hill* coffee table book, the video documentary on The Hill, and of course the tours. "Herny," a nickname he gave himself, is my inspiration to continue the tours or more Hill-related projects. I can only hope I've inspired him to be successful in whatever career path he chooses.

I would be remiss if I didn't mention my wonderful and energetic fiancée Christen Martin, whose coaxing of "Hey Joey, time to stop procrastinating!" kept me on track.

Lastly to all The Hill natives who took the time to review my drafts, those who took or offered pictures, especially The Hill Neighborhood Center and Tracy Duchinsky, plus those who participated in "dry runs," a testimonial to your enduring love of our neighborhood.

# FOREWORD

**Dear friends:**

My mom, Josephine Ann Gianino, was born on The Hill and grew up on Wilson Avenue. She attended St. Ambrose School, received her sacraments at St. Ambrose Church, and married my dad there in 1956. I did not grow up on The Hill, but spent much time visiting relatives, indulging in Amighetti's bread, and attending social events there.

When Archbishop Rozanski called to inform me I was being stationed as pastor of St. Ambrose, I was overwhelmed with the honor of this assignment. When I told the news to my mom, who was not in the best of health, it was the first time in a long time I saw her smile. She is very proud. That was a priceless—priceless— moment for me.

To be here, to see the pride in this community of Italian heritage, to see children walking to school every day, to see the visitors coming from all over the country to visit the neighborhood and St. Ambrose—all of these things tell me that this is truly a special place.

There are three pillars to The Hill: St. Ambrose, the businesses, and the residents. St. Ambrose has been blessed to have many dynamic, hard-working, and wonderful priests— most notably Monsignor Sal Polizzi, who saved The Hill when a new highway was coming in that threatened to divide it, and Monsignor Vince Bommarito, who helped navigate the resurgence of St. Ambrose and The Hill that continues today. The Hill has indeed undergone a renaissance with new construction, new home building, and new businesses coming in. Are there challenges in every community? Of course. One of the important challenges for The Hill is to retain, maintain, and enhance its proud Italian heritage as it welcomes people from all over in an ever-changing world. The Hill is part of the rich tradition of St. Louis that must be honored and known. The self-guided tours that you are about to take will show you this powerful and beautiful community that helps make St. Louis a beautiful place to live, raise a family, grow in faith, and work.

As you tour The Hill virtually with Hill native Joe DeGregorio, you will have the chance to benefit from his incredible knowledge of this community and its history.

I know that you will feel the energy, love, passion, and enthusiasm of The Hill community. The Italians who formed this great neighborhood and parish have a lot of heritage to be very proud of; that pride is evident to this very day.

Welcome to The Hill. Enjoy your tour. I hope you get to enjoy the food. Enjoy the architecture. Enjoy the friendliness. Enjoy the community. Enjoy the Piazza Imo! Enjoy the rich heritage of this part of South St. Louis that is proudly called The Hill.

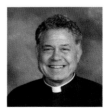

Fr. Jack Siefert
Pastor: St. Ambrose

# INTRODUCTION

CARNIVORE WALL MURAL
TRACY DUCHINSKY

St. Louis's "Piccola Montagna," the highest point in the city, is undergoing yet another renaissance like the one led by legendary Monsignor Sal Polizzi. We are renewing the pride of our Italian heritage, but this time on a different scale. Yes, the pride is still very evident, but now there are many more events and improvements for residents and visitors to enjoy. Besides the traditional church-related gatherings such as St. Joseph's Day, the Corpus Christi procession, and La Festa, this renewed energy has generated annual wine walks, open house tours, outdoor movie nights, neighborhood and school related celebrations at Berra Park, and multiple concerts and chess tournaments at the fabulous new Hill landmark, Piazza Imo. Other 20th-century traditions continue, including the American Legion Easter Egg Hunt, the regional finals of the Soapbox Derby, the Italian Heritage Day parade and festa, Christmas on The Hill, and the now-upscale Giro della Montagna bike race. You will be oblivious to most of the above walking The Hill, but more obvious are the now-numerous younger residents walking by, not to mention the remodeled homes; new, large, modern-but-still-Hill-themed residences; and, on the far east side, many new two-story houses and hundreds of just completed (or soon-to-be completed) luxury apartments. The new and continuing construction, the younger people moving in, all the culinary delights, the forward-thinking residents, the specialty stores, the growing list of activities coupled with the traditional events, and the contagious pride of our neighborhood are fanning the flames of this renaissance, which I began mentioning on tours over 10 years ago. Now you know why I wrote the "bookazine" you hold in your hands. Don't worry—it won't force me out of the tour business, but heck, I am getting older.

Much of The Hill's far west side will not be covered; however, there are some "personalities" who reside there—such as the Gambaro clan of Missouri Baking Co fame; former Mayor of St. Louis, Francis Slay; and my buddy, Keith "Kieto" Ballentine, a colorful figure who decades ago produced dozens of interview and event videos about The Hill. Living in an 1890s log home, he's been a local singer, religious songwriter, and church-service pianist for most of his life

Painfully obvious to long-time Hill residents will be places, pictures, and people left on the cutting room floor by the editing process.

Finally for those who buy this "bookazine" for exercise, there will be a number of "baby steps" followed by a block or two stretch, and be aware that mileage is approximate. Speed reading may help.

Joe DeGregorio

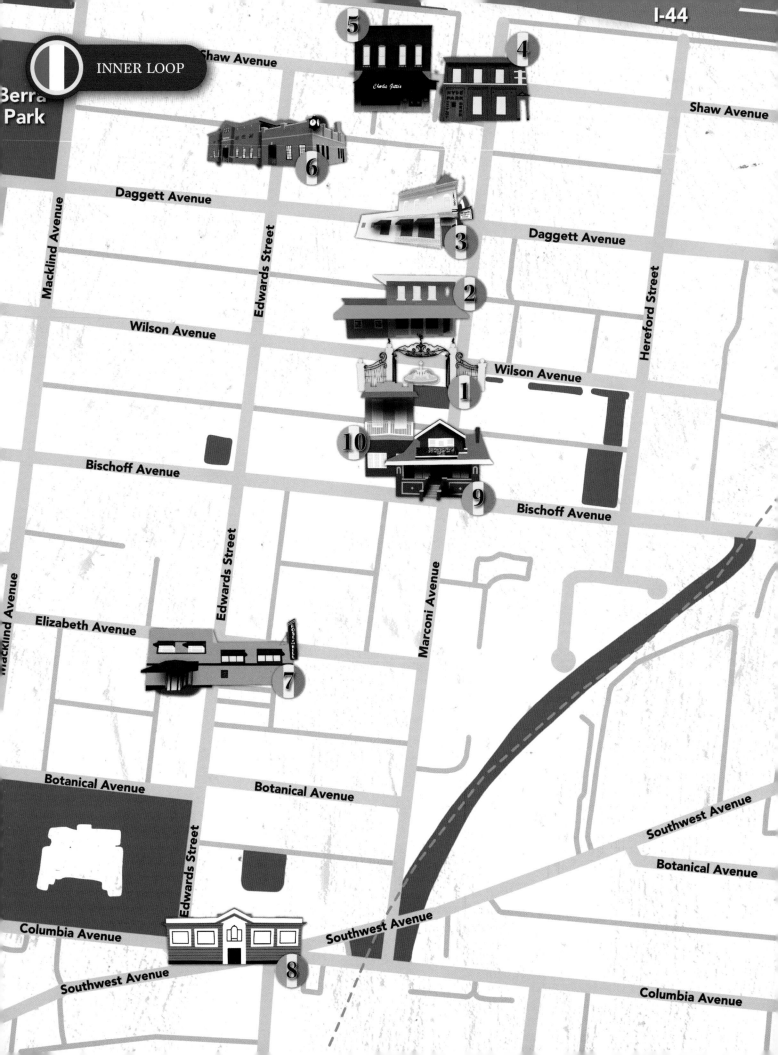

INNER LOOP

Berra Park

Shaw Avenue

Shaw Avenue

Macklind Avenue

Daggett Avenue

Daggett Avenue

Edwards Street

Hereford Street

Wilson Avenue

Wilson Avenue

Bischoff Avenue

Bischoff Avenue

Marconi Avenue

Elizabeth Avenue

Botanical Avenue

Botanical Avenue

Southwest Avenue

Botanical Avenue

Edwards Street

Columbia Avenue

Southwest Avenue

Southwest Avenue

Columbia Avenue

# TOUR ONE:

# INNER LOOP

**1.5+ miles**

**Start at 2109 Marconi: Piazza Imo**

*Parking? Ha! Like in an old European city, park anywhere you can. Avoid the St. Ambrose parking lot on Sunday mornings, in the afternoon on school days, after 4 p.m. on Saturdays, and during weddings, funerals, or other events. The Piazza is usually open from 6 a.m. to 10 p.m. all week, unless the gatekeeper oversleeps. No dogs or coolers. Yes, throw coins in the fountain and make a wish.*

## 1   2109 Marconi Ave.
*Piazza Imo*

PIAZZA IMO ENTRANCE

Since August 2019, the Piazza—like the church, built by the people of The Hill—shows our investment in our neighborhood and is a reflection of how we see ourselves. The Piazza isn't just the starting point for you and thousands of others; this Italian town centerpiece is a place for reflection,

socializing, outdoor classes, concerts, plus wedding and reunion photo-ops. Take time to notice the testimonials dotting the site, including the stunning Italian-made marble fountain.

When my sister Tina canvassed the family for donations to buy a bench honoring our father, Roland (long time mailman and tour guide of The Hill) and our hardworking mama, Victoria, we were all in.

**Go left (north) and cross Wilson.**

## DID YOU KNOW?

Eddie and Margie Imo, founders of Imo's Pizza, acquired the naming rights to the Piazza after significant donations including the front gate complex. After attempts to sell or donate a mistakenly oversized fountain base failed, the piece was buried six feet under the current fountain! The lot, vacant for decades, was used as a fake storefront backdrop for the soccer movie *The Game of Their Lives.*

## 2 5201 Wilson Ave.
*Milo's Bocce Garden*

The most frequented sports bar and hangout in the neighborhood was opened in the 1970s by Hill native Tom Savio. Today it's run by popular local alderman Joe Vollmer and his Hill-born wife Sue (Bartoni). Plenty of outdoor seating flanks two covered 50-foot bocce courts. By the way, most in St. Louis pronounce the game "bowchee." You can hone your bocce skills there, but don't wear dark pants or shoes, as the courts can be dusty.

BOCCE AT MILO'S, C. 1980-90

**Walking north on Marconi from Milo's you will encounter DiGregorio's, but don't walk in yet—it's too early!**

## 3 5200 Daggett Ave.
*DiGregorio's Italian Market*

DiGregorio's exemplifies the American success formula: work hard, plan well, and get a little lucky. This Sicilian-American family emigrated from Europe in the early 1950s and are now in their third generation at the store, with fourth-generation children waiting in the wings.

**Continue north on Marconi and make a left on Shaw, stopping at 5200.**

BIG CLUB HALL, C. 1970
*THE HILL NEIGHBORHOOD CENTER*

## 4 5200 Shaw Ave.
*The Big Club Hall*

First known as the North Italian American Mercantile Company and Co-op in the early 1900s, this was The Hill's first large building and lifeline for newly arrived Lombard Italian immigrants. It offered groceries, job leads, bocce, socializing, and club meetings—all the benefits of a mutual aid society. Later, opening up for all Italians, the Big Club Hall became the place for wedding receptions, concerts, and reunions. Through a child's eyes, I can still see revelers dancing the Hokey Pokey and the Bunny Hop, while in the kitchen the traditional Italian roast beef and ravioli were being prepared—always by the same neighborhood ladies. The current photography studio and videographer owners have vowed to keep this historic site in good condition.

**Going west on Shaw you'll pass Gitto's upscale Italian restaurant that also claims to be the birthplace of toasted ravioli.**

## 5 5226 Shaw Ave.
### *Charlie Gitto's on The Hill*

Contrary to some stories, this restaurant was founded by Charlie Gitto Jr. in 1981 and not his famous father. Gitto's (pronounced "jeetoh") is blessed with many loyal diners and out-of-towners, including celebrities and sports figures.

7 STEPS TAVERN
THE HILL NEIGHBORHOOD CENTER

**Round the corner and go left on Edwards and you'll see the parking lot that was once the Seven Steps Tavern. It was also the headquarters for the 24th Ward Democratic Club, so many a political deal or favor was consummated there. Head down Edwards, stopping at the corner.**

## 6 1922 Edwards St.
### *Pagano Development Office Building*

This office building is a Chris Pagano gem featuring a vintage-style clock that graces the pages of many an article about The Hill. Chris is responsible for several beautiful new homes on The Hill. The lot had remained vacant for decades before the owner accepted Pagano's development plans. The vacant property was temporarily transformed into an outdoor bocce club for a scene in the movie *The Game of Their Lives.*

PAGANO CLOCK+OFFICE
TRACY DUCHINSKY

**Cross Daggett and notice the Volpi interior with hanging salamis. Also check out the beautiful, recently completed mural on the northern outside wall. Continuing down Edwards, notice the home on the east side owned by Sicilian immigrants and adorned with seasonal decorations throughout the year. Crossing Wilson will put you in front of Zia's at 5256 Wilson Ave.**

BACKYARD AND DELLA CROCE STATUES, *TRACY DUCHINSKY*

Adding to the visual "flavor" of your walk, be keen to all sorts of heritage indicators from the painted fire hydrants, banners on light poles, Italian flags, Hill columns at the entrances, and more.

**Continue on Edwards and cross Elizabeth.**

## 7 2300 Edwards St.
### *Rose of The Hill*

This location, with a beautifully maintained interior harkening back to ornate restaurant décor of two generations ago, is a large banquet facility for the Favazza Restaurant family.

Formerly known as Agusti's, and before that, the famous Ruggeri's (voted 16th-best restaurant in the country in 1956), Rose of The Hill has feted many a large get-together, including a yearly gathering of all the Italian clubs of St. Louis.

Continuing on Edwards towards the corner at 5256 Botanical you'll notice a statue of the Blessed Virgin Mary, one of many that dot The Hill. These are a reminder of The Hill's deep Catholic roots. Go south on Edwards and then make a left at the corner in front of what we natives still call "The Columbia Show."

MARY STATUE BY OLIVA
TRACY DUCHINSKY

## 8  5333 Columbia Ave.
*Columbia Foundation for the Arts*

Yes, the exterior of the building still evokes memories of our pre-teen and teen years going to the movies on Friday nights, complete with a dash of social mayhem that owner Bess Schulter and manager Joe Tapella were constantly trying to

COLUMBIA SHOW CONCESSION, 1975
THE HILL NEIGHBORHOOD CENTER

COLUMBIA FOUNDATION FOR ARTS INTERIOR
WEBSITE

quell. The theater had a 50-year run, then briefly became a racquetball center in the 1970s, breathing its last gasp (or so everyone thought) after a disastrous fire in the late '70s. Enter artisan and foundation founder Frank Schwaiger in 1987. Frank transformed this once-grand Hill showpiece into his unbelievably beautiful private residence. In 2019 Frank turned his treasure over to the foundation. Like our Piazza, this art center is one more example of The Hill's surging renaissance.

Continuing east on Columbia and merging into Southwest, make a left on Marconi at popular Favazza's and notice the gargoyles on the Marconi side of the building.

It was once a tavern serving Anheuser-Busch products exclusively; Tony and John Favazza thought the gargoyles would be a fitting nod to the past.

Strolling down Marconi now heading north, take notice of typical "shotgun" homes like the one at 2325 Marconi Ave.

Most homes these days have been, or are being, completely renovated. This home design originated long ago in Louisiana where houses were taxed by width, thus lessening the assessment.

"SHOTGUN" HOUSE
TRACY DUCHINSKY

ROW OF HOUSES ON MARCONI
*MISSOURI HISTORY MUSEUM, ST. LOUIS*

**Continue to the end of the block approaching Bischoff and notice the Colonial style and modern two-story homes on your left.**

PARTY ROOF
*DAVID GRASSI*

The latter was built in two years by a now-retired contractor who was born and raised on The Hill.
Best "party roof" and view in the whole neighborhood! Before crossing Bischoff you'll notice the auto repair business with the name "Fairmount." Fairmount Heights was once the name of the area now known as The Hill.

**Crossing Bischoff and passing a welcoming hair salon (that, of course, was once a tavern), you'll spot the lovely boutique, Koho.**

# 9 2119 Marconi Ave.
*Cielo*

CIELO INTERIOR
*TRACY DUCHINSKY*

Pause at Cielo. Much more than a hair salon, this self-described "urban retreat" offers guided meditation services, hemp treatments, and women's overall health advice. Walking in several times over the years to drop off Hill tour brochures, I have always gotten a sense of peace and contentment. Really!

Years ago, 2119 Marconi was known as the "cheese house" because the owner used the basement to cure many rows of balled cheese, which he then sold.

# 10 2115 Marconi Ave.
*The "Double House"*

Right in front of you is your last stop: a home occupied by a young couple who decided to spruce up the alley side with plants and garden decorations. To their utter surprise, they began to experience the miracle that is the Hill, noticing mostly anonymous floral and decorative "additions" to their beautification efforts, including a painting complete with an easel that disappears right before a storm and reappears afterwards!

**NOW you can head down the block to Gelato Di Riso for a treat.**

# OUTER LOOP

**We start our tour at the place that literally defines what The Hill is all about: The eternal centerpiece of the neighborhood, St. Ambrose Church.**

## 1 Block of 2100 Marconi Ave.
*St. Ambrose Roman Catholic Church main entrance*

ST. AMBROSE, C. 1950
MISSOURI HISTORY MUSEUM, ST. LOUIS

Often described as the religious and community anchor of The Hill, St. Ambrose has seen many Italian, Italian American, and other priests assigned here, proving the church's role as the cornerstone of The Hill over the past 119 years. Assigned in 2021, new Pastor Fr. Jack Siefert is fully aware of the challenge and is very much up to it. Older and now-deceased Hill residents started their life journey with baptism, confirmation, and marriage within The Hill-made brick walls of this historic edifice. Using the Basilica of St. Ambrose in Milan (the city's Patron Saint) as a guide, architect Angelo Corrubia designed this Lombard Romanesque masterpiece, which was dedicated in 1926 and cost $150,000.

The five-bell church tower on Wilson is almost an exact duplicate of St. Ambrose's bell tower in Milan. Feel free to start your walk slowly while gazing at the Italian and American flags, the memorials at your feet, and the *Italian Immigrants*

statue on the left, designed by renowned sculptor Rudy Torrini. Looking closer at the statue you'll see a note on the husband's lapel, on which is written the family name, Italian city of origin, and "St. Louis," so folks in New York could put them on the right train. If the church is open with no events scheduled, feel free to take in the awe-inspiring interior.

**Heading north on Marconi and crossing Wilson, you'll see what I will always call "The Amighetti Bakery Building," even though the bakery closed a while ago.**

### DID YOU KNOW?

My father, sickly at birth, was rushed to the still-under-construction St. Ambrose for an emergency baptism in the basement, which served as the temporary church. They stopped wedding, baptized Dad, and the bride and groom became the godmother and godfather. Yes, my father Roland was THE original wedding crasher! And, ironically, my Aunt Jo Signorino was the first one baptized in the newly dedicated church.

AMIGHETTI'S BAKERY
THE HILL NEIGHBORHOOD CENTER

CALCATERRA FUNERAL HOME
THE HILL NEIGHBORHOOD CENTER

I remember Mom asking me to buy a loaf of still-warm bread after Mass. But she would always give me enough money for two, knowing I would eat one on the way home.

◐————————————————

**Continue on Marconi past Herbaria, to 2008.**

## 2 **2008 Marconi Ave.**
*So iLL*

The former Spielberg Furniture store, So iLL is definitely not your mother's fashion accessories and showroom store. Here since 2021, this internationally acclaimed producer of trendsetting rock-climbing apparel, holds, and accessories is worth a walk through. The name "So iLL" represents owner Dan Chancellor's southern Illinois roots.

◐————————————————

**Look to your right when crossing Daggett to see Calcaterra Funeral Home, another example of the "everything you need is right here" environs. Continuing on Marconi, notice the building at 1926, which was once the Sicilian "Palma Agusta Club."**

## 3 **5147 Shaw Ave.**
*Shaw's Coffee, LTD*

At the northeast corner of Shaw, the "Riggio Bank Building," played a major role in helping new Italian immigrants, just as other benevolent societies like the Fratellanza Society did. Starting as a hardware store in 1906, in 1921 the Riggio brothers—Ignazio, Joseph, and Frank—built this structure, purposing it for currency exchange, real estate, insurance, and travel arrangements. It also served as a base for charity and humanitarian efforts via Mrs. Anna Riggio. My mom, Victoria, lived upstairs in the 1930s and '40s.

RIGGIO BUILDING
TRACY DUCHINSKY

◐————————————————

**Head west on Shaw after crossing Marconi, taking in the former Giovanni's restaurant, the Victorian-style home, and many shotgun homes.**

On the spot where the new townhomes stand, neighborhood kids used to stage nickel-a-ticket summer musicals.

**Continue to 5257 Shaw.**

## 4 5257 Shaw Ave.
*The Fair Mercantile Building*

Built by the Paul family in 1920 to sell furniture and appliances, this was a go-to place for immigrants, similar to Speilbergs. My sister Fran and Hill native Toni Venegoni, along with

FAIR MERCANTILE ORIGINAL SAFE
TRACY DUCHINSKY

future TalentPlus modeling owner Sharon Tucci, handled the sales registers there in the 1960s. My sister recalled, "The Paul brothers were funny people but also sticklers for balancing the day's receipts to the penny. Not balancing meant not going home until reconciled." So the "three amigas" kept a secret $2 slush fund to ensure an on-time departure.

**Stroll down Shaw until the I-44 overpass comes into view.**

## 5 5300 block of Shaw Ave.
*The Interstate 44 overpass*

You won't see any markers or plaques here, but this is perhaps the site of The Hill's greatest triumph. During the uproar over the ultimately unavoidable tragedy of plowing through the neighborhood instead of redirecting a few hundred yards north, The Hill lost 100 homes during the I-44 construction in the late 1960s and early '70s. Just as sad was the predicament of the 100 or so homes remaining on The Hill's northern tier connected only by a pedestrian walkway. A committee was formed (headed by Msgr. Polizzi) of politicians and others to petition for an overpass allowing emergency vehicles quicker access along with easier resident access to amenities south of I-44—including, of course, St. Ambrose. Despite being offered $50,000 raised by the neighborhood in seed money, state and federal entities turned down the proposal. That is, until then Secretary of Transportation John Volpe jumped in after conferring with President Nixon and declared, in essence, "Keep your $50 thousand. You will have your overpass." The story made national news, including *Time* magazine, and Msgr. Polizzi was later named one of the top 100 young leaders in America.

**Continue down Shaw, cross Macklind making a left toward Berra Park.**

## 6 1825 Macklind Ave.
*Berra Park*

BERRA PARK SIGN
THE HILL NEIGHBORHOOD CENTER

Playing soccer on frozen turf; endless summers of horseshoes; the board game "Mill;" pickup games of baseball, softball, or football; "Undoon" the snow cone man; watching night softball leagues hoping a player cracks a bat so you can tape it up to use later; and so many festivals. These are The Hill memories of Berra Park. Created decades ago from marshland, this joyful gathering place has seen great improvements in the last 25 years. There's now a new pavilion, a modern playground, and beautiful landscaping. The park is named after the first Italian-American elected city office holder, Midge Berra. Feel free to walk the rectangular perimeter and create memories of your own.

Cross Daggett and note at 2129 a plaque honoring church musician and instructor Charlie Garavaglia. Head south crossing Daggett, Wilson, Bischoff, and Dempsey, and pause at Elizabeth.

You'll pass notable places like Anthonino's Taverna and plaques noting prominent Hill personalities including poet and prolific writer Eleanor Berra Marfisi and the home where Jack Buck's family once resided, near the corner at Elizabeth. By the way, this is the only block in America where three baseball Hall of Famers once lived. Also by this time you'll have noticed the uphill climb. The dome of the state building you see ahead of you is the highest point in the city of St. Louis. Hence, the rationale for calling this area "The Hill."

## DID YOU KNOW?

On a future stroll check out The Hill's north side past Highway 44. Note that a private residence on the 5300 block of Northrup was, in 1890, an African American school named Cheltenham (later renamed Vashon after the school's first principal, John B. Vashon). Also on Northrup are two Volpi salami factories, one cures 400,000+ prosciuttos every day! A must see at 5025 Pattison is the tourable Chocolate Chocolate Chocolate Factory. Nearby on 1711 Hereford is Pete's Bakery, which caters to commercial outlets, and the venerable Pop's Blue Moon at 5249 Pattison, formerly Papa Prost, a cozy dive with live music and roots back to 1908.

**Continue south on Macklind and look to your left at Columbia.**

## 7 5329 Columbia Ave.
*Shaw Visual and Performing Arts Elementary School*

Henry Shaw Elementary School became a tuition-free alternative to parochial school for some Hill children in 1907. Back then, high school wasn't an option for most kids, since supporting the family was the priority. In the 1950s, the school was designated an after-school community activity center with a variety of classes for children and adults. As the current name for the school implies, the school's curriculum draws students from all over the city.

SHAW SCHOOL, C. 1952
MISSOURI HISTORICAL SOCIETY, ST. LOUIS

**Continue on Macklind, crossing Columbia to the corner of Macklind and Southwest.**

Before crossing Macklind and making a left, note the tavern-like building catty corner that is now a private social club for current and former St. Louis–area soccer players. Continue east, noting the Hanneke Hardware sign, a lasting memorial to the family that catered to Hill and Southwest Garden residents for many decades. Down by The Hill Cigar shop are Southwest Auto Parts and Columbia Auto Repair across Southwest. If you spot owner Joe Barbaglia, say, "Hi Mayor!" as he's known as The Hill's de facto mayor. The business has been locally owned since 1938.

Continue to the stoplight and cross Southwest. Turn right and cross Marconi by Favazza's. Turn left heading north and notice the still active, early 20th century railroad tracks below the bridge.

Pass the Favazza's parking lot. On the 2300 block of Marconi is the almost block-long former McQuay Norris Foundry, built over 100 years ago to supply the burgeoning St. Louis auto industry with piston rings and chassis parts.

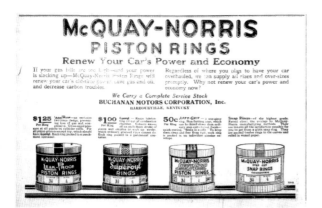

MCQUAY-NORRIS AD

### 8  2300 block of Marconi Ave.
*The Hill's very own "business park"*

Over the years, multiple businesses located or relocated here. The largest portion belongs to DiGregorio's Market warehouse where, as I say on my tours, "There is more pasta and sauce stored there than you will see in your lifetime."

### 9  2210 Marconi Ave.
*Italia-America Bocce Club*

Founded in 1975 and moving into the former offices of the McQuay-Norris Foundry in 1993, this private club boasts 440+ members. Once described by a visiting California bocce player as one of the best and most beautiful clubs in

## DID YOU KNOW?

PRESIDENT CLINTON AT BOCCE CLUB, 1996
MISSOURI HISTORICAL SOCIETY, ST. LOUIS

Bocce was NOT invented in Italy but in Egypt over 7,000 years ago. The club hosts the American Bocce Federation's national tournament every four years and instituted a gratis after-school high school league. During a St. Louis stop in the 1990s, President Clinton was taught the game of bocce by club veterans.

America, the club has multiple women's and men's leagues, social events, and tournaments throughout the year. As a member, I've been allowed to bring tour groups in for bocce history, lessons, and to play on the five international- standard 82-foot-long courts. The club's spacious banquet hall has been the site of countless celebrations.

**Cross Bischoff, walk down a few doors, and notice a beautiful European-style home before 2018 Marconi.**

The last building by the alley, now a private residence, my mom said it once housed the neighborhood library, which she frequented. My dad agreed, but added, "Library, yes, but during Prohibition there was a casino in the back!"

**Time to double back to Vitale's Bakery or fast forward to DiGregorio's to get your Hill fix.**

# TOUR THREE

# FOODIE
## PHASE ONE

**1.6+ miles**

**Start your walk at the corner of Marconi and Bischoff and head north.**

## 1  2130 Marconi Ave.
*Vitale's Bakery*

ANGIE VITALE

In 1976, Grace (Bommarito) and her husband Pete Vitale moved her grandfather's business from its downtown location to The Hill. Pete's bakery is now run by third-generation siblings, Angie, Sam, and Michael, with the fourth generation waiting in the wings. Offering a vast array of Italian cookies and breads, Vitale's also offers Sicilian cannoli, touted by many as The Hill's best. 65,000 pizza shells and 750,000 loaves of bread go out the door to clients every week! Among the most popular: Sicilian-style bread and St. Louis-style gooey butter cookies. Check out the locally famous, weather-protected Blessed Virgin Mary statue on the roof. There were several businesses on the site prior, including Campisi's grocery store.

**Passing the church and across Wilson stands what many here still call "Amighetti's," even though the business closed in 2019 after a controversial media-covered dispute between the franchisee and the copyright owner.**

## 2  5141 Wilson Ave.
*Former Amighetti's Bakery*
### 2028 Marconi Ave.
*Sandwich Shop*

AMIGHETTI BAKERY
THE HILL NEIGHBORHOOD CENTER

The bakery, started by immigrant Louis Amighetti Sr. in 1917, moved to this location in 1921. And the sandwich shop became nationally famous in the 1970s for their "Amighetti's Special" sandwich.

## 3  2024 Marconi Ave.
*Pizzeria da Gloria*

Formerly the site of Amighetti's overflow area and opening in 2020, owner Lou Kurowski uses an authentic, Italian-made, wood fired oven for his unique crispy pizzas, created with homemade sauce, sausage, and even stracciatella. My favorite? Pizza da broccoli rabe & sausage.

Looking right across the street is Milo's, a sports bar/restaurant run by popular Alderman Joe and his wife Sue (Bartoni) Vollmer.

## 4 5201 Marconi Ave.
*Milo's Bocce Garden*

Considered the most popular social gathering place on The Hill, Milo's boasts ample indoor and outdoor seating, excellent casual Italian and American food, and two 50-foot bocce courts made of crushed oyster shells and clay, so don't wear dark clothes when playing. Not to be missed are the grilled grouper and the large variety of wings. Since 1902 The Hill has been home to 35 or more taverns. As Merlo's this location was Anheuser-Busch exclusive; later it was "Toots" Pezzani's Wil-Mar Lounge. Milo's was founded by prior owner Tom Savio. The hands-on Vollmers first started as half-owners in 1989.

Across Wilson to the left is home to the most authentic Italian gelato around.

## 5 5204 Wilson Ave.
*Gelato Di Riso*

Owner Larry Fuse Jr. offers a variety of delicious flavors churned from an Italian-made machine. Many customers who have visited Italy depart with gelato déjà-vu. The name "Riso," meaning "rice," is a reference to the previous owner's last name. However, there is in fact a rice-based gelato made in Florence.

REMAINS OF OVEN
*TRACY DUCHINSKY*

## DID YOU KNOW?

Each February, Milo's hosts a "Polar Bear" Bocce Tournament. Beer is available, but bring your own gloves. When owned by the religious Mr. Merlo, he would insist customers halt imbibing whenever the church bells pealed.

100 years ago, the building housed communal bread-baking ovens.

Go east on Wilson, then cross Marconi heading down the block passing some colorful homes to Dominic's.

## 6 5101 Wilson Ave.
*Dominic's on The Hill*

Elegant and intimate with classic Florentine décor, Dominic's regional Italian cuisine has earned many four-star honors and media accolades.

Debuting in 1971, Sicilian-born Dominic Galati completed his dream of owning an upscale Italian restaurant. His Italian wedding soup has been donated to many a St. Joseph Day culinary feast held at St. Ambrose. Singer Tony Bennett was once a frequent customer when in town for concerts.

Groundbreaking Andrino's was previously at this location, ushering in an era of more upscale restaurants in addition to the venerable Ruggeri's (covered on page 34).

DOMINIC'S RESTAURANT
TRACY DUCHINSKY

**Turn left on Hereford, and notice all the new homes and apartments across the street.**

## 7 5100 Daggett Ave.
*J. Devoti Trattoria*

Initially named Five Bistro and opening in 2006, this establishment was the realization of chef/proprietor Anthony Devoti's dream of bringing to The Hill a farm-to-table fine-dining restaurant with ever-changing menus and Italian overtones. The pride in preparing their own pasta, meats, condiments, and other essential ingredients translates into delicious and often unique

ANTHONY DEVOTI WITH VINTAGE PIC
TRACY DUCHINSKY

offerings. Look in the back yard by his vegetable gardens, and you will spot his very own bee farm/honey-making operation! This was once the site of two venerable cafeteria-style diners, Cassani's and Galimberti's. The smells of the Friday fish and pasta dishes or the barbecue plates still linger in the minds of many a Hill-raised baby boomer.

**Cross Hereford.**

## 8 5048 Daggett Ave.
*Charlie's Market on The Hill*

In March of 2020, Steve, Matt, and Jim Imo, nephews of Ed Imo, founder of long-time pizza chain, Imo's Pizza, decided to open a deli to complement their Imo's Meat and Sausage Company, founded in 1971 in the same building by their father, Charlie. Top choices here are the family recipe Hot Salami or Charlie's Special sandwiches. Of course, Provel cheese is a staple here. For out-of-towners taking the walk, Provel cheese is a whole other story you can learn about on my culinary tour.

**OK now, try to keep your mind off eating and keep walking. This time, cross Daggett and turn right, heading east until you reach Rigazzi's.**

## 9 4945 Daggett Ave.
*Rigazzi's*

The oldest still-operating restaurant on The Hill, Rigazzi's has been feeding customers American-Italian family-style pairings since 1957. Returning older customers wax nostalgic remembering family visits there to fill up prior to Cardinals or Blues games. Time travelling to the typical Italian mid-20th century eateries, the interior is covered with a multitude of artifacts, statues, and pictures. The traditional buffet style lunch harkens back to the days of feeding nearby factory workers. Oh yes, and you can still get their famous Frozen Fishbowl of beer. If you drink one now, you're totally done walking.

RIGAZZI'S VINTAGE
THE HILL NEIGHBORHOOD CENTER

## DID YOU KNOW?

St. Louis–raised actor John Goodman frequents Rigazzi's when in town. My dad and I met him there once, with Goodman touting how great The Hill is. The name "Rigazzi" is a combination of the family names of 1957 owners "Riganti" and "Aiazzi." The idea for a fishbowl was inspired by the shape of a beer schooner offered during the 1904 St. Louis World's Fair. Behind Rigazzi's used to be an ice-cream-cone factory, no doubt also inspired by the 1904 World's Fair.

**Farther down the block at 4915 Daggett is the location of Oliva on The Hill, which includes a banquet center, an outdoor garden area, a lunch spot, popular "Wine Down Wednesdays," a growing antique market, and a B&B owned by Mark Erker and Carleen Kramer.**

Worth a look if sticking around later. Sala's Café was on this site from 1911 to 1976, feeding Hill residents and factory workers.

**Before heading north on Boardman to make a left toward Guido's on Shaw, you'll see the brand-new Moda luxury apartments to the south, and yes, they'll have plenty of parking!**

## 10  5046 Shaw Ave.
*Guido's Pizzeria and Tapas*

Opened in 2000, Guido's boasts of offering "A taste of Spain in the middle of Italy." It features authentic, quality Spanish and Italian dishes, notably seafood paella and award-winning pizza.

Run by Miguel Carretero with work ethic, restaurant prowess, cooking, and recipe inspiration from the restaurant's founders, father Segundo and mother Genoveva who still show up to work there. The family emigrated from Spain to St. Louis in 1970, and The Hill is glad they did.

## DID YOU KNOW?

Segundo Carretero returned to Spain after waiting tables at the 1964 New York World's Fair Spanish Pavilion and came to St. Louis after the Pavilion was moved here in 1969. Guido's is the favorite Hill dining spot for St. Louis radio personality and local historian, Ron Elz (a.k.a. Johnny Rabbit). The site once housed Cassani's sporting goods store and Frank Lo Piccolo's tavern.

As you walk west toward 5141 Shaw, you'll be passing the residence (not disclosed for privacy) of the late Rich LoRusso, a gregarious Hill icon whose wife Terri still runs the award-winning LoRusso's Cucina near The Hill. The LoRussos have been generous supporters of Hill fundraisers for over 40 years. The cioppino at LoRusso's is not to be missed.

## 11   5101 Shaw Ave.
### *Adriana's on The Hill*

Catty corner from Guido's, Adriana's opened in 1992 as a lunch-only café. Adriana Fazio, with the help of her daughters, was determined to create a menu replete with real, homemade, Sicilian-style, casual cuisine.

ADRIANA WITH CAPONATA
*TRACY DUCHINSKY*

But to really dip into the Sicilian mode, you must try their eggplant appetizer, Caponata.

MRS. RUMBOLO
*THE HILL NEIGHBORHOOD CENTER*

Former Pentagon and CIA director Leon Panetta was once spotted there getting his Southern Italian fix. Hill favorite Rumbolo's grocery store and sandwich shop graced this corner for decades.

## 12   5139 Shaw Ave.
### *J. Viviano & Sons*

VIVIANO OLIVE TUBS AND PRICEBOARD
*TRACY DUCHINSKY*

Starting out in 1900 as Viviano Bros. Macaroni Company, the family enlarged their 1950s Hill Italian grocery market in 1979, which today is run by third-generation John Viviano and brother Tony. If viewing through the storefront windows makes you think, "This is the way Italian grocery stores looked 100 years ago," you would be right. Gazing inside at the thousands of imported Italian items stacked all over the place will complete your time-travelling fantasy. Mama Mia!

The wine specials, the stuffed grocery cart sales, the rows and rows of all kinds of pasta, and the one-of-a-kind Italian specialties combine to create a vintage mood that is punctuated with occasional concerts by the Viviano's Louie Prima–sound-alike cousin, Tony Viviano.

John has expanded his deli business and tripled the interior seating capacity. His grandfather, store founder John Viviano, was rescued from the sinking Italian luxury liner

ANDREA DORIA

*Andrea Doria* in 1956 on a return trip from Italy. A picture of the ship still hangs on the west wall of the store.

## 13 5147 Shaw Ave.
*Shaw's Coffee LTD*

Founded in 1999 by Walter and Gail Boyle, this former Riggio bank building showcases their high-quality micro-roasting process.

Peeking through the window reveals the stately relaxing décor, ample greenery, and the large coffee bean-roasting equipment. You should also try the house-made pastries.

As Riggio for most of the 20th century, it was a place where immigrants obtained loans, established savings accounts, found housing, got legal advice, prepared for citizenship, and even purchased steamship tickets. Shaw's Coffee even retained the original safe deposit vault as a seating area.

SHAW'S COFFEE LTD
SHAW'S COFFEE

## DID YOU KNOW?

The 1874 structure at 5201 Shaw, probably built by German immigrants, was once the location of DiMartino's Italian Restaurant and before that, DiMartino's Italian Grocery store. My mother, Victoria, was born upstairs.

As Giovanni's restaurant, Giovanni Gabriele was picked by President Reagan's 1980 Inaugural Committee to create a pasta dish to be served to 4,000 people. Guess who raved about the *farfalle con salamone* the most? Attendee Frank Sinatra, who insisted the dish be named "farfalle con salamone à la Presidente Reagan!"

DIMARTINO'S ITALIAN RESTAURANT
*MARIE DIMARTINO WOHLERT*

**Cross Marconi**

## 14 5201 Shaw Ave.
*Sado (Coming Soon)*

In a surprise (for The Hill) development, the former Giovanni's restaurant has been transformed to an upscale Japanese sushi restaurant named "Sado," which means "tea ceremony." Chef Nick Bognar and his father

Michael have promised to support Hill activities and hinted at creating an "Italian-Japanese" dish or two. Noodles anyone?

◑ ——————————————————————

**Crossing Shaw to head south on Marconi, you'll see on Shaw a former major social, reception, and co-op building, built initially for Lombard immigrants and described as "Big Club Hall."**

Now housing primarily a photography business, you may ask, "What's the foodie walking tour connection?" In its 125-plus-year history there've been tons of ravioli, beef, polenta, bread, salata, and who knows what else served there during the thousands of parties, wedding receptions (including Yogi Berra's), and meetings held there. No doubt culinary ghosts permeate every square foot. In 2022, the Italian Club of St. Louis held their 100th anniversary dinner there as a tribute.

COOKS IN THE BIG CLUB HALL
THE HILL NEIGHBORHOOD CENTER

## 15 1913 Marconi Ave.
*Marconi Bakery*

Originating in 1918 as a bakery owned by the Lupa family, the tradition continued with Sam Licata in 1968 and the business is now operated

CIAO CHOW COOKIES
TRACY DUCHINSKY

by the DiGregorio family. Sam still works there part time. The store still uses Old World traditions and recipes to make speciality breads for in-store customers plus Southern Italian–style breads for city-wide distribution. Under Licata, the site became a hangout for the "Sunday Morning Club," which included Ronnie Purcelli, Joe Grasso, and many others.

## 16 1923 Marconi Ave.
*Ciao Chow*

Opening in July, 2021, this first-on-the-Hill pet food store is owned by Jessica Mastrantuono-Hellmann, who loves to talk about her homemade Italian-themed dog biscuits, especially canine favorite, doggie cannolis.

A portion of the profits go back to their partnered pet rescue organization, All Paws Safe Haven. Before Ciao Chow, an upscale antique store prospered on this spot. Berra Furniture Store was the site's business throughout most of the last century. The tiled Berra name still graces the front entrance.

## 17 1927 Marconi Ave.
*Bertarelli Cutlery*

Starting their business in 1967 and moving to this location in 2003, the Bertarelli family hails from a long line of "moletas" (knife sharpeners) rooted

BERTERELLI KNIVES

in northern Italy. A popular store city-wide, the cutlery services a significant percentage of area restaurants and stores. But excellent knife sharpening isn't all they handle these days. You can even take landscaping equipment there for refurbishing. Reconditioning or selling upscale culinary equipment, and, more recently, getting into the medical supplies and commercial paper products arena is more proof of the enterprising spirit this family forged long ago in the hills of northern Italy.

## DID YOU KNOW?

There are two ancient pushcart knife sharpeners displayed in the storefront windows. I remember as a child the "klink clank clunk" sound the pushcart would make as a local moleta, Tony Gagliarducci, made his rounds.

Phyllis Florist, once here, was a go-to place for weddings, funerals, and special occasions. In 1965, I got a gorgeous orchid arrangement for my prom date and Sam said to me, "Ok kiddo, you have a great time tonight and no charge this time."

**As you walk past The Hill Neighborhood Center, know that in there somewhere are stacks of books, magazines, and memorabilia that collectively contain thousands of recipes.**

Before you cross Daggett, glance to your left and take in Café Dolce, 5143 Daggett Avenue, owned by Aggie Santangelo, giving the neighborhood another popular, cozy place to socialize while enjoying high-quality European-style coffees and pastries. You justa gotta try their Genoa cannoli cookie!

CAFE DOLCE INTERIOR
TRACY DUCHINSKY

## 18 5200 Daggett Ave.
*DiGregorio's Italian Market*

Celebrating its 50th anniversary in 2021, this family-run enterprise is the epitome of the

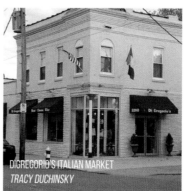

DIGREGORIO'S ITALIAN MARKET
TRACY DUCHINSKY

American success story. Voted Best Artisan Shop along with many other honors, they offer a mind-boggling array of homemade

VINTAGE DIGREGORIO'S MARKET
*THE HILL NEIGHBORHOOD CENTER*

products, imported Italian foods, and Italian wines. Work ethic coupled with dedication to all Hill-related activities make this establishment a great place to get your Italian fix.

This was once the site of popular nightclub Savoy Gardens. The building's south side once contained a small theater built in the 1920s. DiGregorio's has sponsored several spaghetti-eating contests over the years—fun to watch and gruelingly messy as a participant.

◐ ————————————————————————

**Continue down the west side of Marconi, but notice on the east side, Herbaria, makers of**

HERBARIA
*TRACY DUCHINSKY*

herb infused, essential oil soaps. You'll be able to smell the scents from across the street.

## 19 2016 Marconi Ave.
*Herbaria*

"A homemade soap store on a foodie walk?" you may ask. Why not? And where else could I put it? Besides, half owner and founder Ken Gilberg says mice loved to dine on his products until they were all evicted! With over 60 varieties of plant-based products and a variety of related offerings, your skin can't go wrong. This folksy and friendly spot is run by Melissa Gibbs and Blake Larson, who will be delighted to give you a tour that includes a definitive history of soap-making.

The building was once an addition to the adjacent Spielberg's Furniture Store, and a mysterious tunnel was built underneath joining both buildings.

VINTAGE SPIELBERG OWNERS
*THE HILL NEIGHBORHOOD CENTER*

◐ ————————————————————————

**This concludes this portion of the foodie walk. If not already starving from the sights and smells incurred, feel free to begin the foodie tour in the next chapter.**

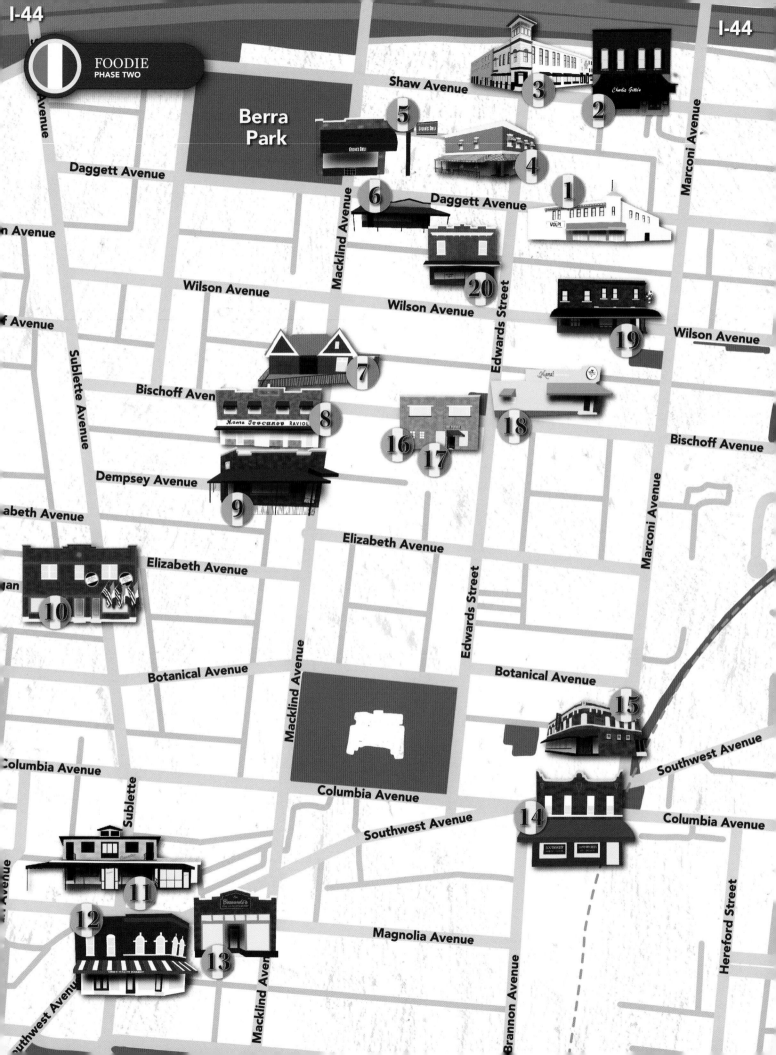

# FOODIE
## PHASE TWO

**1.8+ miles**

**Begin your walk at Milo's Bocce Garden, 5201 Marconi, and head west on the north side of the 5200 block of Wilson passing signature "shotgun" homes.**

*Imagine all the wonderful Northern and Southern Italian–style home-cooked meals prepared here over a span of over 120 years.*

**Make a right on Edwards, heading north one block until you get to 5256 Daggett.**

## 1 5256 Daggett Ave.
### *Volpi Foods*

LORENZA & ARMONDO PASSETTI
VOLPI

Without a doubt, Volpi's is the largest manufacturer of ANYTHING on the Hill. Started in 1902 by Milan immigrant John Volpi, this maker of artisan meats now encompasses four factories, three of them on The Hill. Volpi's ships its products all over the world. On any given day, around 400,000 prosciuttos are curing, a multiple month process. They use the same centuries-old traditional methods and recipes Mr. Volpi brought to St. Louis in 1899, and the company has spanned over four generations of family ownership. It is currently under the leadership of Volpi's great-niece Lorenza Pasetti. The family has always had high quality and safety standards, making it well suited for today's strict regulatory environment. Taking a peek into the retail store and deli gives you a tip-of-the-iceberg look at their operations.

**Walk up one block north on Edwards, crossing Daggett, and stop briefly at the corner parking lot. The 7 Steps Tavern was here once, and a lot of political deals were made in the smoke-filled back rooms. Make a right (east) on Shaw.**

## DID YOU KNOW?

Volpi's takes pride in hiring workers from diverse backgrounds, especially recent immigrants and refugees. When providing a tour once to 65 students from Beijing, China, I asked Volpi's if they could provide salami samples. They happily provided the students with salami they sell to China, complete with ginger!

## 2 5226 Shaw Ave.
### *Charlie Gitto's on The Hill*

Opened in 1981, Gitto's has been a beacon for those looking for fine dining and superb service. Starting with the eggplant appetizer and moving down the menu, every dish is a bit of culinary heaven. On a warm summer evening, the outdoor garden provides a *Roman Holiday* experience. The restaurant was featured in a 2019 *New York Times* piece on St. Louis by Jane Smiley, who admitted that she was not expecting to be impressed. But after the signature toasted ravioli, her first bite of filet Siciliano "nearly knocked [her] out of [her] chair." How about that for a favorable review!

### DID YOU KNOW?

Before Gitto's, Angelo's, a venerable pasta and steak house, kicked off the toasted ravioli controversy. Proprietor Angelo Oldani claimed toasted ravioli was invented at his place when a chef accidently dropped ravioli into frying oil. Charlie Gitto and his staff promote this version of the appetizer's creation to this day. However, there is another nearby restaurant making the same claim, thus stirring up a great tempest in a hot oil pot that the media exploits from time to time. My take? Fuggettabout it!

CHARLIE GITTO'S
*TRACY DUCHINSKY*

OK, reverse course and backtrack to Edwards. Across the street on Shaw, notice the former Fair Mercantile furniture store, now the site of Carnivore and various businesses.

## 3 5257 Shaw Ave.
### *Carnivore*

The latest Italian steakhouse and banquet center, Carnivore delivers as expected. But "no forgetta to mangia da pasta." Co-owners and workers Mike and Casie (Yogi Berra's great niece) Lutker and Joe and Kerri Smugala have the place managed by another of Yogi's great-nieces, Danielle Brown. Feeling adventurous? Try the Luganiga Sliders. The what? Trust me, a delish Northern Italian sweet breakfast sausage, not anything weird—look it up. There is a colorful mural on the interior wall that depicts almost all of the businesses on The Hill.

Cross Edwards and make a left, staying on the west side of the street until you reach 1933 Edwards.

## 4 1933 Edwards St.
### *Lorenzo's Trattoria*

FAMILY DINING ROOM IN THE KITCHEN
*MAUREEN FUSE*

Lorenzo's takes pride in serving Northern Italian cuisine, just as owner Larry Fuse Jr. takes pride in his Lombard roots. This culinary style emerged in Lombardy from large dairy and pig farms (cheeses and salami), rice paddies (risotto dishes), potato farms (Northern Italian–style gnocchi), and wheat fields (specialty breads, tortellini, and ravioli). Any of his other Italian-style dishes are worth a visit too, but first timers should start with any of Larry's famous risotto offerings.

**Turn right and head west on Daggett until reaching Gioia's. Notice the shotgun homes with unusually large front yards.**

## 5 1934 Macklind Ave.
*Gioia's Deli*

If you haven't yet tried a hot salami sandwich, you haven't really experienced all that is the Hill. This northern Italian boiled specialty made of beef, pork, and spices was once known as "Salame de Testa." The Gioia brothers started out with a grocery and deli in 1918. The Donley family took over in 1980, winning the nationally prestigious James Beard Foundation award in 2017. The deli also offers other Italian- and American-style sandwiches. Suggestion: For your first hot salami, skip all the condiments except mustard to have a "purer" experience.

## 6 5356 Daggett Ave.
*Gian-Tony's Ristorante*

As Lorenzo's is authentic Northern, Gian-Tony's is award-winning authentic Southern. It's operated by Sicilian native Tony Catarinicchia, son Rosario, and his daughter Liz. For starters, try the Italian wedding soup, followed by your favorite appetizer and just about anything else. My favorite? The

AGUSTI'S RESTAURANT, NOW GIAN-TONY'S
THE HILL NEIGHBORHOOD CENTER

Sicilian Pasta Milanese. This corner had several tenants over the years, including Lance Berra's, Pastori's, and Agusti's.

**Going south on Macklind, you'll pass the former Club Casino, which once offered Italian and American food, dancing, and a lot of liquid refreshments. Crossing Wilson, you see Sacred Heart Villa day care center, where Sister Felicetta churned out her homemade pasta to raise funds. Walk further to arrive at the corner of Macklind and Bischoff, and you'll see a gas station that's not a gas station.**

## 7 2130 Macklind Ave.
*Pit Stop*

Formerly a gas station owned by Bob Zone, Debbie Rizzo's Pizza Place, J. Smug's GastroPit, the Smugala family, and owners of other casual eateries

around metro St. Louis, the Pit Stop has been reincarnated to include salads, bowls, wraps, fried chicken, and other comfort food. With childhood memories of watching cars repaired and the smell of grease guns, I'm glad this now 100-year-old edifice was never torn down.

*STL TOASTED IN 2023!*

# 8 2201 Macklind Ave.
## *Mama Toscano's*

VINTAGE ITALIAN HERITAGE PARADE BY MAMA TOSCANO

Catty corner from the Pit Stop, Mama Toscano's has made labor-intensive homemade ravioli for four generations. The business is on hiatus for now. Their ravioli recipe called for 10 ingredients, and they were a long-time media darling of the Food Network and other culinary sites.

# 9 2225 Macklind Ave.
## *Anthonino's Taverna*

Up the block, still heading south, is a very popular "split personality" restaurant. Half Greek and half Italian brothers Anthony and Rosario bring out their heritage in a creative menu.

ANTHONY SCARATO
PIC OF FIERI
*TRACY DUCHINSKY*

Recommended are the oversized, hand-made, toasted ravioli (which was featured in Guy Fieri's *Diners, Drive-ins and Dives*) and the spanakopita. Pizza? Try the thick version, voted the best many years in a row.

---

**Traverse on Macklind, making a right at 5400 Elizabeth and noting the plaques by the street of Jack Buck, Ben Pucci, Yogi Berra, and Mickey and Joe Garagiola (covered in Tour 5).**

Here are two Yogi Berra food stories: Home for lunch one day from Shaw School, Yogi's nieces were surprised to see the New York Mets team that Yogi then managed eating hearty portions of salami, provolone, hot salami, and Italian bread. Niece Mary Frances hurriedly captured autographs on napkins, later selling them for a nickel each. And when Yogi couldn't get back to town, he didn't let that keep him from getting some home cooking. The former manager of Oldani Salami factory would get a mysterious call every February to send crates of salami to a Florida location. She finally figured out it was Yogi's way of preparing for spring training.

---

**Cross Sublette, making a left to cross Dugan.**

# 10 2321 Sublette Ave.
## *Joe Fassi Sausage and Sandwich Factory*

This establishment was named after the family's patriarch and has been operated by a Fassi or family member since 1926. Relative Tom Coll has been serving quality sandwiches here—including Aunt Jennie's Salsiccia Stinger—since the early 1990s. Decorating the walls are family and Hill sports nostalgia pictures and articles. At one time it was an Italian-American Tom Boy brand grocery store, with Emil Fassi's tavern next door. I vividly remember as a child going with a list and telling Mary Fassi to put the tab "on the books."

VINTAGE: PAUL, JOE EMIL AND VINCE FASSI
*PAULA FASSI*

At 12 years old, my first job ever at Fassi's paid 25 cents an hour and involved stocking shelves, making sausage, and dressing chickens and rabbits in the basement.

**Walk on Sublette, crossing Columbia, and then cross the street at Magnolia.**

## 11 5453 Magnolia Ave.
*Cunetto House of Pasta*

This restaurant opened in 1974 when Hill pharmacists Vince and Joe Cunetto got into the business after rave reviews of the meals they fed local doctors and travelling salesmen. Run for decades now by Vince's son Frank, Cunetto's remains an iconic and popular place for delicious and plentiful family recipe dishes. There may not be a better dish on all The Hill than Cunetto's signature linguini *tutto mare*, a shellfish, broth, butter, and garlic masterpiece.

**Continue on Sublette about 100 feet crossing Southwest making a left.**

## 12 5430 Southwest Ave.
*Urzi's Italian Market*

Urzi's interior transports you to the 1920s era of its founding. Each shelf, nook, and cranny reveals another variety of pastas, Italian culinary basics, souvenirs,

URZI FAMILY WITH CANNOLI
*TRACY DUCHINSKY*

kitchenware, and their famed spice collection. Novice and seasoned chefs alike are amazed at how much "good stuff " owner Diane Urzi and third-generation daughter Rosa have lovingly crammed into tight spaces. On my culinary tours, Diane creates and provides the history of the world-famous Sicilian dessert, cannoli.

## 13 5424 Magnolia Ave.
*Lou Boccardi's Restaurant*

Although it is right next door to Urzi's, the slight bend in the street puts Boccardi's on Magnolia. The Boccardi family of restaurants are famous for their delicious pizzas; owner Lilly Boccardi does it all, and be sure to try their original cannoli ice cream, introduced in 2019.

**Continue east on Southwest, passing the Hanneke Hardware sign and the under-construction Amighetti's sandwich shop. Pass The Hill Cigar Shop that boasts "You can bring your own lunch." At the stoplight, cross the street towards Southwest Market.**

## 14 5224 Columbia Ave.
*Southwest Market Cuisine*

A great place for casual Italian and American food. You can't go wrong with the signature Po' Boy, but try the option of building your own sandwich, Dagwood-style!

**Cross Southwest at the light and take a right heading east.**

## 15 5201 Southwest Ave.
*Favazza's Restaurant on The Hill*

FAVAZZA'S OUTSIDE
PAUL DEGREGORIO

Owners Tony and John Favazza owe a lot to parents Vito's and Ellen's family recipes and restaurant know-how. Also benefiting is Tony's head-chef son, Mark. The addition of European-style outdoor seating a few years ago brings the capacity, including their Rose of The Hill banquet center, to about a thousand. Delicious and plentiful cuisine (recommendation: the chicken Sicilian), long term, friendly employees, and the utmost efficiency makes Favazza's a good stop for any size group.

————————————————

**Turn left on Marconi, go two blocks, then turn left on Elizabeth; now go right on Edwards and cross over to the west side of the street, proceeding north to Salumeria Oldani and Eovaldi's Deli.**

## 16 2201 Edwards St.
*Salumeria Oldani's*

Same mailing address, but different businesses. A "life comes full circle" story, Leo Oldani's Italian Salami started in the late 1940s here after current owner Marc Buzzio's father taught Leo in New York the thousand-year-old method of dry-curing meats. Owned for seven years by local Charlie "The Salami Guy" Oldani (not related to Leo), the business was eventually sold to Marc.

VINTAGE OLDANI SALAMI
THE HILL NEIGHBORHOOD CENTER

Making artisan products like wild boar and truffle salamis for high-end restaurants in New York and New Jersey, Marc had to prove to a leery USDA in 2003 that dry-curing the old-world way was still safe. This venerable process makes Oldani's one of the more interesting culinary tour stops.

## 17 2201 Edwards St.
*Eovaldi's Deli and Catering*

Take a peek in the window for another of many vintage Italian delis on The Hill. Eovaldi's is always in the running in the "best deli" category, thanks in part to the potato salad and also the "Sicilian Bomber"—with Tums as dessert. Currently, Eovaldi's and DiGregorio's are the only places you can purchase nostalgic Oldani's salami. The store's several owners over the years include Sam Rumbolo and his son Joe and retired St. Louis Police Lt. Johnny Carnaghi.

## 18 2132 Edwards St.
*Mama's on The Hill*

Stroll across the street to the only seven-day-a-week lunch and dinner restaurant on The Hill, run by hands-on owner Andrea Ervin and daughter Lauren. Take a recommendation from

MAMA'S ON THE HILL
TRACY DUCHINSKY

the Food Network and order the pasta with rabbit Bolognese sauce. The adventurous can try Mama's "Pasta Challenge," a two-pound meatball lying on an enormous pile of red sauce spaghetti, with no tab if you can finish in an hour. *Buona fortuna* with that! This is one of two locations claiming to be home to the accidental creators of toasted ravioli. In this version of the story, in the 1940s a slightly inebriated bartender/cook nicknamed "Fitz" dropped a ravioli order in the boiling oil instead of boiling water by mistake.

## 19 5256 Wilson Ave.
*Zia's On The Hill*

BAR AT ZIA'S
TRACY DUCHINSKY

One block north of Mama's is a restaurant whose name means "aunt" in Italian. Run by the Chiodini family since 1985, this hometown favorite is always busy. Their version of St. Louis-favorite Chicken Spiedini is as good as it gets. They might also have the best sweet Italian salad dressing in St. Louis. You can't go wrong with a combination of quality and quantity here. When the food-truck craze took hold 15-plus years ago, Zia's was St. Louis's first restaurant to take part. For decades, the building was home to Consolino's grocery store.

## 20 2027 Edwards St.
*The Missouri Baking Company*

"What's a chocolate drop?" you ask. Shaped like a round, flat, chocolate-covered doughnut with

MISSOURI BAKING COMPANY
TRACY DUCHINSKY

pound-cake qualities, this sweet has delighted five generations of Hill children, producing almost sacred memories. It has been a fixture at family gatherings, reunions, and weddings, and it's still a must-try for the present generation of The Hill's young ones. This 1924 neighborhood bakery—in reality a regional institution—is run by third-generation siblings Chris Gambaro and his gregarious sister, Mimi Lordo. Be warned before peeking in the window to view the pastries, Italian cookies, and bread: your self-guided tour is likely to take a 20-minute detour. Then again, this is your *last* stop, so you might as well indulge!

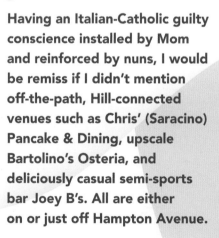

**Having an Italian-Catholic guilty conscience installed by Mom and reinforced by nuns, I would be remiss if I didn't mention off-the-path, Hill-connected venues such as Chris' (Saracino) Pancake & Dining, upscale Bartolino's Osteria, and deliciously casual semi-sports bar Joey B's. All are either on or just off Hampton Avenue.**

The HILL

Northrup Avenue

Northrup Avenue

Macklind Avenue

Marconi Avenue

I-44

I-44

Pattison Avenue

I-44

Shaw Avenue

Shaw Avenue

Hereford Street

Berra Park

21

Macklind Avenue

Daggett Avenue

20

22

1

2

3

Wilson Avenue

19

Edwards Street

Wilson Avenue

6

Bischoff Avenue

5

4

17

18

8

7

Bischoff Avenue

Dempsey Avenue

16

11

9

13

15

14

Elizabeth Avenue

12

10

Marconi Avenue

Botanical Avenue

Botanical Avenue

Edwards Street

Southwest Avenue

Macklind Avenue

Southwest Avenue

Columbia Avenue

## TOUR FIVE

# PERSONALITIES

**1.9+ miles**

**Start at 1919 Marconi. A "charming" aspect of The Hill—park wherever you can, but try not to take up storefront spots.**

*The Hill, like many St. Louis neighborhoods, has always been replete with personalities. Yogi Berra and Joe Garagiola top many lists, of course. Our St. Louis Soccer Hall of Famers are included, and Msgr. Sal Polizzi deservedly achieved national recognition.*

In addition, you will get to know other Hill achievers and some "characters" in this section. Most of these deserving folks have been made famous in the media, but a few are immortalized by old-fashioned handed-down stories and Hill-only articles. Fourteen are honored with sidewalk plaques sponsored by and paid for by our fantastic neighborhood association, Hill 2000, in their Walk of Fame program. A prime example of a local personality is Joe Barbaglia, our de facto "Mayor," who is involved in everything.

A group of 1966–69 St. Ambrose graduates called "The Hill Boys" are dedicated to assisting the church and community any way they can.

FATHER SIEFERT WITH HILL BOYS GROUP

My dad, Roland DeGregorio, who spent 25 years as The Hill's "postino" (mailman) and 25 years as a Hill tour guide was like most of his WWII-era neighbors and friends—totally committed to the neighborhood. Many more deserve recognition, but then you'd be stopping at every third house!

## 1 1919 Marconi Ave.
*Frank Borghi*

Borghi traveled the familiar path of area soccer players from the 1930s to the 1970s, starting on local teams, progressing to sponsored elite amateur teams, and later joining professional leagues, national tournaments, soccer-centric universities, the Olympics, and World Cup soccer. Check out the plaque on the sidewalk nearest the street. Borghi was also the longtime director of the Calcaterra Funeral Home half a block away. Soccer was not generally played by first-generation immigrants, as it was a game for the elites in Italy back then.

FRANK BORGHI ON LEFT
*THE HILL NEIGHBORHOOD CENTER*

At the 1950 Soccer World Cup in South America, the little-regarded US team bested powerful England 1-0 in a preliminary round at 70-1 odds. It is still considered the biggest upset in World Cup history. Goalie Frank Borghi, along with other Hill players featured later, is prominent in Geoffrey Douglas's Game of Their Lives book and the subsequent movie. Frank is in the National and St. Louis Soccer Halls of Fame.

**Turn around and go south on Marconi. Take a left on Daggett, bypassing (for now) the wonderful Café Dolci coffee shop. Stop in front of 5119 Daggett.**

## 2 5119 Daggett Ave.
*Frank "Pee Wee" Wallace*
Playing forward for local teams, Frank was also a member of the 1950 US World Cup Soccer team and earned berths in the National and St. Louis Soccer Halls of Fame.

US WORLD CUP TEAM
THE HILL NEIGHBORHOOD CENTER

## DID YOU KNOW?

Nicknames, especially for boys, were very popular during much of the 20th century. Wallace's nickname was earned because he was short and skinny as a kid. Hill author and poet Eleanor Berra Marfisi penned a colorful book on mostly WWII-generation neighborhood nicknames titled *Soprannomi*.

**Cross the street and walk to 5108 Daggett.**

## 3 5108 Daggett Ave.
*Gino Pariani*
Gino, also a member of the famed 1950 World Cup team, played for the US in the 1948 Olympics and is in the US National and St. Louis Soccer Halls of Fame. His wedding was moved up so he could play on the World Cup team.

## 4 5100 block of Wilson Ave.
*Gina Galati*
*(Specific address not provided for privacy.)*
On this street lives the most talented soprano operatic singer residing in St. Louis. Hill braggin' rights are in effect here for sure, but I dare you to find one better. Gina is now well into her second decade of managing Hill headquartered Winter Opera St. Louis, which she founded. Besides nationwide appearances, her local venue also hosts fundraisers, solo appearances and dinner shows at her father's restaurant (Dominic's), and the Christmas on The Hill concert at Piazza Imo.

GINA GALATI, CENTER, HOLDING A BOOK
GINA GALATI

## 5 5110 Wilson Ave.
### *St. Ambrose School*

VINTAGE ST. AMBROSE SCHOOL
*THE HILL NEIGHBORHOOD CENTER*

Safely crossing to the south side of Wilson, you'll be in front of the school, whose roots go back to 1906. The current building, completed in 1949, certainly has had its share of personalities over the years among the dedicated nuns, lay teachers, and staff. Talk to any school alum from 14 to 100 years old, and you will hear individual stories, some hilarious, but all appreciative of school staff efforts.

**Continue on the south side of Wilson, reaching 5130.**

## 6 5130 Wilson Ave.
### *St. Ambrose Church Rectory*

This is the primary address for St. Ambrose Church, which is confusing since the church

## DID YOU KNOW?

St. Ambrose was established in 1903 to serve the Italian Roman Catholics immigrating here primarily to work in the clay mines and brickyards. The original wooden structure was destroyed by fire in 1921.

ST. AMBROSE, C. 1903
*MISSOURI HISTORY MUSEUM, ST. LOUIS*

MSGR. SAL POLIZZI, YOGI BERRA, CARMEN BERRA, AUDRIE GARAGIOLA, JOE GARAGIOLA, & MSGR. BOMMARITO DURING HALL OF FAME DAY

entrance is on Marconi. Historically, the rectory housed many dedicated priests. In the recent Reedy Press publication The Hill: St. Louis's Italian American Neighborhood and the award-winning documentary America's Last Little Italy: The Hill, well-deserved accolades were given to Msgr. Sal Polizzi, who rejuvenated the neighborhood's pride in its Italian roots during the late 1950s to early '80s, and Msgr. Vincent Bommarito, who oversaw the current renaissance until his departure in July 2021. Now there's a new sheriff in town, Fr. Jack Siefert. "Siefert"? A priest with a German name on The Hill? Well, you're half right—the other half is Sicilian. Is he conflicted? You bet! Hill connection? His mother, a Gianino, lived in the neighborhood. A passionate combination of love, ambition, historical awareness, and religious fervor, Fr. Jack is the perfect priest at this juncture of The Hill's saga. If you see him walking the grounds with his dog or riding his electric cart, by all means, introduce yourself to this very approachable spiritual leader of the parish.

**Continue walking on Wilson, and just before approaching the *Italian Immigrants* statue, look down at a plaque honoring Seaman Mario L. Bazzetta, the first of 23 Hill natives to make the ultimate sacrifice in World War II, in this case at Pearl Harbor on December 7th, 1941.**

**Go left (south) at the church, crossing Bischoff to 2210 Marconi.**

### 7 2210 Marconi Ave.
*The Italia-America Bocce Club (IABC)*
*Aldo Della Croce*

One of the premier private bocce clubs in America, the IABC hosts the national tournament every four years. The club now boasts over 440 members, and there are scores who have contributed significantly to its success since 1975. None, however, are more revered than founding father Aldo Della Croce, a stone-carving artisan in his own right with statuary and pillars adorning the club. Aldo promoted bocce and the club so well that a major annual tournament is named for him.

**Double back and cross Bischoff (named after a German scientist by early arriving German immigrants), going left (west).**

### 8 5200 block of Bischoff Ave.
*The DiMaggio Family*

*(Specific address not provided for privacy).*
Notice the beautiful, modern, Italian-style, brick and stone-front shotgun homes on the street. Also living on the block is a family typical of successful younger people recently moving here. Loving the environs, the DiMaggio family has quickly made a positive impact, with husband Jay a productive board member of The Hill 2000 neighborhood association.

**Passing 5225 on Bischoff, know that the garage housed a fully functional blacksmith shop until just a few years ago. You can still see the blacksmith's handiwork in the wrought-iron fences dotting the neighborhood. Make a left on Edwards until reaching the large building at 2300.**

The Favazza family's Rose of The Hill was once Henry Ruggeri Sr.'s renowned restaurant, rated 16th-best in the country in 1956. Hundreds of entertainment, sports, and other celebrities visited during Ruggeri's 75-year reign. Many Hill personalities worked there, including Yogi Berra and Mickey Garagiola, my dad, and yours truly.

My fondest memory came at nine years old while (sort of) helping my father do inventory. I strayed into the kitchen and was astonished to see a three-foot-tall birthday cake. "Whose birthday?" I asked. The chef replied, "Laraine Day." My dad later described her as a Hollywood movie star meeting up with husband, Hall of Fame baseball manager, Leo Durocher, in town playing the Cardinals.

### 9 2301 Edwards St.
*The Ruggeri House*

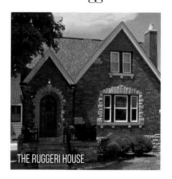

THE RUGGERI HOUSE

This house was built by a wing of the family who managed Ruggeri's restaurant, and whose son, Robert Ruggeri, became a highly respected alderman from 1981 to 1999. A masterful politician known for promoting community stability, Bob was witty, engaging, and proud of his Lombard heritage. A street in the new La Collina housing development is named for him.

### 10 2307 Edwards St.
*Marie "Re" Calcaterra*

A couple of doors down is the former home of Marie "Re" Calcaterra. Marie helped pioneer the

## DID YOU KNOW?

Living in the immediate area are Chris and Joan Saracino. Joan regularly helps at Hill events and Chris is currently president of the Hill 2000 neighborhood association, guiding the neighborhood to many successful improvements over the years. And as the longtime president of the Hill Business Association, Chris accomplished similar feats.

sport of synchronized swimming, training many champions. She would later be inducted into the International Swimming Hall of Fame. See the plaque on the sidewalk.

**Turn back to Elizabeth and make a left until you reach Macklind, but not before noticing the well-kept "retro style" brick homes circa 1930s and, across the street, a preserved early Fazio Bakery storefront.**

## 11 2300 area of Macklind Ave.
*Mike Santangelo*

Ok, you've been trekking The Hill for a while and haven't seen or heard anyone really acting "Italian-American" as depicted in movies or TV shows. Here's your chance. Meticulous about his landscaping, Mike is therefore outside often. If you see him, go up and say (with cupped fingers, Italian style) "Hey! I'm on a Joey De self-guided tour, and he wants to know 'How youuu doin'?!'" The response should be hilarious. Mike, the former president of the Sicilian Cultural Association, runs an Italian-American oriented radio program and assists with Hill events. He

continues to make a positive impact for the St. Louis Italian community.

St. Louis Soccer hall of famer John Pisani lives just up the street. He was president of the former Business Men's Club of The Hill, which awarded scholarships to deserving college-bound students for over seven decades. John, along with his brother Paul, also a St. Louis Soccer hall of famer, were also skilled professional painters, tapped several times to touch up the interior of St. Ambrose, just as their father did. Paul played on the US soccer team in the 1964 Olympics in Tokyo.

## 12 5405 Elizabeth Ave.
*Jack Buck*

Built in the late 1920s by successful businessman John Ferrara Sr., this two-story brick duplex was one of the larger homes on The Hill at the time. One of Ferrara's sons, John Jr. was co-founder of the Pasta House Company along with Kim Tucci and Joe Fresta.

In 1954, just after being hired as a broadcaster for the St. Louis Cardinals, easterner Buck was advised that a nice home on The Hill was available. No doubt that when Buck realized this was the same block where Yogi Berra and Joe Garagiola grew up, the choice was a no-brainer. Besides announcing for the Cardinals from 1954 to 2000, Jack also covered eight World Series and 17 Super Bowls. He was inducted into several sports-related Halls of Fame, most notably in Cooperstown. Note the plaque honoring him on the front sidewalk.

JACK BUCK

**Continue down the street until reaching 5447.**

## 13 5447 Elizabeth Ave.
### *Lawrence Peter (Yogi) Berra*

What can one say about a homegrown, worldwide phenomenon? A lot! One of the best baseball catchers ever. Ten World Series rings. A Hall of Famer with three MVPs. The most famous malapropist in recorded history. As down-to-earth and dedicated to giving back as they come.

JOE GARAGIOLA AND YOGI BERRA (BOTTOM RIGHT) CHILDHOOD TEAM
*THE HILL NEIGHBORHOOD CENTER*

**Walk to the end of the block by Sublette Avenue (named for the wife of a famous fur trapper), making a left across Elizabeth and turn left again until you reach 5446.**

## DID YOU KNOW?

Berra's real nickname growing up was "Lawdy." His mother, Rosa, running out of family boy names after having three older sons, named him Lawrence but couldn't pronounce it. Surprisingly, the best athlete in the family was an older brother who had to work in local factories to help support the family. As a Navy man in World War II, Yogi steered a rocket launcher ship during the Normandy invasion. He was thrilled when beautiful, smart waitress Carmen Short fell in love with a goofy-looking guy like him. Many Italian-Americans around the country assumed Yogi had Southern Italian roots, but he was of Lombard heritage, as was Joe Garagiola. Visit the Yogi Berra Museum and Learning Center on the Montclair University Campus in New Jersey. Living in Montclair since 1948, Yogi was best known as a long-time catcher for the New York Yankees even though his initial aspiration was to be a Cardinal. When he wasn't offered a signing bonus like his best friend Joe Garagiola, Yogi opted for the Big Apple.

## DID YOU ALSO KNOW?

The two most-quoted "Yogi-isms" are, I believe, "It ain't over 'til it's over" and "When you see a fork in the road, take it." Here's one that isn't in the books: one of Yogi's nieces, Mary Frances (who now resides in the home—also a B&B) was trying to help Yogi remember the St. Louis hospital where his oldest son, Larry, was born. He kept describing the hospital as "Christian or Catholic." Trying to jog his memory, she responded with several local names—St. Mary's and St. Anthony's. Suddenly Yogi jumped up, saying "Wait, I remember. It was Barnes-Jewish hospital!" Laughing hard, Mary Frances declared, "I have my very own Yogi-ism!"

JOE, YOGI, AND THEIR WIVES AT HALL OF FAME CEREMONY
THE HILL NEIGHBORHOOD CENTER

## 14 5446 Elizabeth Ave
*Joe and Mickey Garagiola*

Literally right across the street from Yogi's house, it's the only home in the neighborhood with two plaques on the sidewalk. Joe and Yogi were lifelong best friends. His best quote might have been, "Not only was I not the best catcher in the Major Leagues, I wasn't even the best catcher on my street!" Joe had an amazing life, not only as a professional baseball catcher for his hometown team and others, but also as a Hall of Fame baseball announcer, 10-year host of the *Today Show*, game show host, sub on the Johnny Carson Show (once having Hill natives Yogi and entertainer Toni Carroll on the same show), and philanthropist (while living his last 20 years in Arizona he renovated an Indian reservation school sports complex and introduced real nuns there!). Joe travelled the country warning youngsters about the dangers of chewing tobacco. Always bragging about his 'hood, he came back to The Hill often, especially during reunions of his club, the Fawns. Joe's older and just-as-talkative brother, Mickey, was

MICKEY GARAGIOLA
THE HILL NEIGHBORHOOD CENTER

very well-known, in part due to his 45 years as a waiter at Ruggeri's, where he fed loyal customers and occasional celebrities with insider baseball info allegedly from brother Joe. Mickey became a local celebrity himself as TV announcer for *Wrestling at the Chase*, the subject of a 2021 book by Ed Wheatley.

## 15 5430 Elizabeth Ave.
*Ben Pucci*

A contemporary of Yogi and Joe, Ben was a gentle giant and excellent athlete whose passion was football. He played for several NFL teams as a tackle, most notably for the 1948 undefeated league champion Cleveland Browns with future legendary Notre Dame football coach Ara Parseghian as his teammate. Ben went into the transportation industry, eventually managing a trucking firm in San Antonio, Texas.

PUCCI (MIDDLE TOP, WITH GLASSES) WITH YOGI AND JOE G., 2003

**Proceed down the block to the alley noting the beautiful brick corner home with a Spanish tiled roof and locally made wrought iron fence.**

This was the home of John and RoseMarie Bianchi, who, almost 50 years ago, founded the Sick and Elderly Program of The Hill. Continued today by their children Bob and Debbie with the help of their own kids, the program provides deserving neighbors with wheelchairs, canes, special bedding, and much more. When my medical insurance wouldn't cover a wheelchair for hip replacement surgery, my dad said "Just ask them." To this day, I remain very grateful.

**Head north (left) on Macklind and make a left on Dempsey on the Anthonino's side (north) side of the street to 5421 Dempsey.**

## 16  5421 Dempsey Ave.
*Toni Carroll*

TONI CARROLL
THE HILL
NEIGHBORHOOD CENTER

Born in Lombardy, Italy, as Lorraine Iadreschi, she moved to The Hill as a child in the 1920s. After attending Washington University's music school, she headed to New York to make a name for herself—and succeeded, to put it mildly. She was a Copacabana and Latin Quarter singer/dancer, international singing star with a million-selling record album, movie actress, model, successful oil wildcatter, cruise ship owner, author, and video producer, and she is an inspiration to everyone she's met.

**Head back to Macklind; make a left crossing Bischoff, making a right on Macklind. Head east on Bischoff.**

### DID YOU KNOW?

Toni met many celebrities in her career. Frank Sinatra, upon learning of her Hill upbringing, remarked, "St. Louis, eh? Volpi salami, the best." Gertrude Merlo, a neighbor across the street who remembered her, said she was very talented. Quite the personality herself and a contemporary of Yogi Berra, Gertrude always told my passing tour groups, "Yogi? He was dumb as a fox and always tried to copy my homework!"

## 17  5337 Bischoff Ave.
*The former Garanzini family home*

Lester and Lee Garanzini's second son, Sam, continues to make an impact on the regional restaurant scene as long-term vice president of the Pasta House Company. The oldest son, Jesuit priest Michael, is a positive force in the scholastic and religious world. At the helm of Loyola University in Chicago for 11 years, he is credited with making major academic improvements, growing the student population, and increasing donor support.

Today Fr. Michael is president of the Association of Jesuit Colleges and Universities and chairman of the board for the International Association of Jesuit Universities. This

FORMER GARANZINI FAMILY HOME
TRACY DUCHINSKY

brilliant but humble man is a great source of pride for those who know his achievements, especially The Hill's baby boomer generation.

Continuing down Bischoff, notice the unique Pagoda-style apartment building at 5319, built in the 1920s. Rollo-Calcaterra, named for WWI and WWII heroes, has been the home of American Legion Post 15 at 5307 Bischoff since 1946. Make a left on Edwards, crossing Wilson, and making another left. Of course you can't miss the brand-new Italian-style townhomes on the south side.

## 18 5300 block of Wilson Ave.
*Jeff Cacciatore*

*(Address not disclosed for privacy.)* On this block, you will pass the home of St. Louis Soccer Hall of Famer Jeff Cacciatore. After excelling at Southern Illinois University soccer, Jeff went on to play for the North American Soccer League. In the '80s, he played for the Major Indoor Soccer League's St. Louis Steamers which fielded many home-grown players. Jeff's boomer generation, including his

JEFF CACCIATORE
GETTY IMAGES

brothers Steve and Chris, contributed as much to the prowess of St. Louis soccer as the generation before. Jeff continues to teach youngsters the finer points of the game to this day.

Notice the beautifully restored and new family homes on both sides, including that of everybody's friend, Derio Gambaro.

A successful businessman, Derio has contributed to the betterment of The Hill and church in every way imaginable. For example, he's been president of

# DID YOU KNOW?

During a St. Ambrose grade school soccer game, my father and soccer coach, recalled grade-schooler Jeff running toward him in tears as the opposition was roughing him up on the field. After reassuring Jeff for a few minutes and making sure he wasn't hurt, Dad, a grizzled World War II Marine Corps vet, told him to get out there and attack. Jeff never looked back and maintained his hovering, close-in attack style throughout his career.

the St. Ambrose Grade School Alumni Association for decades, which puts on an all-class breakfast reunion every May. Derio was elected to the Missouri legislature in addition to serving on the state Board of Education.

At the end of the block is the one-time Club Casino, a hopping joint through the mid-20th century that attracted young people from all over. Cross Wilson at Macklind, noticing the Sacred Heart Villa, the expansive playground, and the beautiful Blessed Virgin Mary Grotto, site of many a pageant. Stop by the plaque at the entrance.

SACRED HEART VILLA

## 19   2108 Macklind Ave.
*Sister Felicetta Cola ASCJ*

SISTER FELICETTA COLA ASCJ
THE HILL NEIGHBORHOOD CENTER

Just as much of the world loved and respected Saint Mother Teresa of Calcutta, The Hill reveres the memory of Sister Felicetta. Upon her arrival at the Villa in the 1940s, she became a pioneer of its early childhood development program. Every child was special to her, and her service spanned several generations.

**Double back to the corner, cross Macklind heading west (left), and then cross Wilson heading north.**

## 20   2005 Macklind Ave
*Eleanor Berra Marfisi*

A retired high school principal, Eleanor become known as one of the most prolific writers about The Hill and our Italian roots in its 130 plus year history.

The most popular of her creations was titled, *The Hill: Its History–Its Recipes* which included one of my all-time favorite dishes, Dominic's *zuppa di pesce* (fish soup). Eleanor's works covered such diverse topics as Hill nicknames and remembering cherished aspects of our Italian born "nonnas" such as their use of garlic as a healing remedy. Her book, *Sicily: Crossroads of Culture*, really piqued my interest, since I am of Sicilian descent.

## DID YOU KNOW?

The intersection of Macklind and Daggett near the Marfisi home is the finish line for the annual Soap Box Derby The Hill has hosted since 1977.

---

After Daggett (named after the fifth mayor of the city of St. Louis), turn around and look up Macklind, pondering the upward slope ending at Arsenal. The dome you see is the highest point in the City of St. Louis. At this juncture you should be saying to yourself, "Aha . . . that's why they call it The Hill!"

## 21   1825 Macklind Ave
*Berra Park*

Most newcomers and visitors initially assume the park was named after our famous export, Yogi Berra. But smack in front of you is a bust of Louis G. "Midge" Berra, the park's real namesake. The well-respected Berra is noted as the first Italian-American to be elected to city-wide office as Collector of Revenue. "Midge" was a nickname he got because he was small as a kid. He later sprouted, but the name stuck. He also owned the Brass Key, a popular nightclub at the site where Cunetto's House of Pasta now stands.

---

**Cross Macklind again, heading right (east) on Daggett, pass the home of John and Jane Torretta (address not disclosed for privacy), yet another cog in the wheel of dedicated Hill**